A HISTORY
OF PICTURES

FOR CHILDREN

DAVID HOCKNEY
& MARTIN GAYFORD

A HISTORY OF PICTURES

FOR CHILDREN

From Cave Paintings to Computer Drawings

ILLUSTRATED BY Rose Blake

Abrams Books for Young Readers, New York

Published by arrangement with Thames and Hudson Ltd. London

A *History of Pictures for Children* © 2018
Thames & Hudson Ltd

Texts by Martin Gayford © 2018 Martin Gayford
Texts by David Hockney © 2018 David Hockney
Works by David Hockney © 2018 David Hockney
Illustrations by Rose Blake © 2018 Rose Blake

Abridged and adapted by Mary Richards
from *A History of Pictures* by David Hockney
and Martin Gayford
Book design by Sarah Praill

First published in the United Kingdom in 2018 by
Thames & Hudson Ltd, 181A High Holborn, London WC1V 7QX

Library of Congress Cataloging-in-Publication Data:
Names: Hockney, David, author. | Gayford, Martin, 1952—
author. | Blake, Rose, 1987— illustrator.
Title: A history of pictures for children : from cave paintings to
computer drawings / by David Hockney and Martin Gayford ;
illustrated by Rose Blake.
Description: New York : Abrams Books for Young Readers, 2018.
| Includes bibliographical references and index.
Identifiers: LCCN 2017058996 | ISBN 978-1-4197-3211-9
(hc-pob with jacket)
Subjects: LCSH: Art—History—Juvenile literature.
Classification: LCC N5308 .H63 2018 | DDC 709—dc23

10 9 8 7 6 5 4 3 2 1

Printed in China by Shanghai Offset Printing Products Ltd.

Abrams Books for Young Readers are available at special
discounts when purchased in quantity for premiums and
promotions as well as fundraising or educational use. Special
editions can also be created to specification. For details, contact
specialsales@abramsbooks.com or the address below.

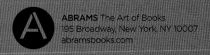
ABRAMS The Art of Books
195 Broadway, New York, NY 10007
abramsbooks.com

CONTENTS

INTRODUCTION

Pictures are all around us: on laptops, phones, in magazines, newspapers, and in books like this one. We can see them on the streets and on TV. They hang on the walls of our homes and in art galleries and museums. It is through pictures just as much as words that we think, dream, and try to understand the world around us.

This book is based on many conversations I've had with my friend Martin Gayford, who writes about art. So it contains two voices. As you read you'll know who's speaking, as our names are written next to our words. There's a third person in the conversation, too: our illustrator, Rose Blake. She's drawn pictures of the three of us on the pages. Sometimes you'll spot my pets and other artists in her pictures, too.

I'M DAVID HOCKNEY AND I AM AN ARTIST. I MAKE PICTURES. I DRAW, PAINT, TAKE PHOTOGRAPHS, AND CREATE WORK USING COMPUTERS AND TABLETS. WHILE I'M DOING THIS, I ALSO LOOK CAREFULLY AT THE WORK OF OTHER ARTISTS, AND DISCUSS ART WITH OTHER PEOPLE.

— DAVID

This book isn't written like a traditional history (in which you might expect to discover the order in which things happened), but if you turn to page 118 you will find a timeline. This shows what tools artists were using and how their work was affected by new inventions. There's also a glossary on page 122, where you can look up any words you may not already know.

The pictures I like might be quite different to the ones you'd choose if you were writing your own story of pictures. As you read the book (or as someone reads it to you), talk about what you can see. When we look at pictures, we all bring our own points of view; that's one of the great things about art, and why I keep making it.

—David Hockney

MARTIN

Rose

THINKING ABOUT PICTURES
Why do we make pictures?

DAVID: Pictures are very old. They may even be older than language. I like to imagine that the first person to draw an animal was watched by someone else, and when that other person saw the creature again, they would have seen it a bit more clearly.

When we create pictures, we must look closely. The artist who painted a bull on the wall of a cave in Lascaux in southwestern France around 17,000 years ago must have looked at the creature very carefully.

Drawing of a bull, Lascaux cave, France, c. 15,000 BCE

PABLO PICASSO *The Owl*, 1952

Every picture ever made has its rules. Someone has put it there, and arranged it so it would cover a certain area. When the Spanish painter Pablo Picasso created this picture of an owl in 1952 he made it according to his particular point of view.

We all see the world in our own way. Even if we are looking at a small, square object—let's say, a box—some of us will see it differently from others. When we go into a room we notice things through the lens of our own feelings, memories, and interests.

MARTIN: When we look at art, we often try to answer two questions: Why was this image made and what does it mean? You also have to ask yourself: What's in the picture? In Egyptian art the biggest figure is the pharaoh. Look at this picture of Pharaoh Ramses II, painted on a temple wall in the 13th century BCE. Of course, if you had measured him in real life, he would have turned out to be the same size as anyone else, but in the Egyptians' minds he was bigger, so that is how he was painted.

DAVID: Throughout time, artists have searched for different ways to translate our world, which is three-dimensional, onto a flat surface like a piece of paper or canvas. In that way, a picture can be compared to a map. The task of a map maker is to describe the features of a curved object—the Earth—on a flat one. It's impossible to do this precisely! So we can say that all maps reflect the interests and knowledge of the person who made them. It's the same with pictures.

MARTIN: Looking at the history of pictures, you notice connections between images that come from very different times and places. Two people in a room, a view out of the window, a pet: these can be found in Jan van Eyck's *The Arnolfini Portrait*, and also in your painting *Mr and Mrs Clark and Percy* (on the next page) painted more than 500 years later.

Van Eyck was working in the Netherlands in the 15th century. His pictures were fresh and new, and looked very different than the ones other artists were making at the time. By layering oil paint, he created deep, rich colors and delicate details. He painted this picture of Giovanni Arnolfini, a merchant from Bruges, and his wife in 1434.

DAVID: Van Eyck's paintings are full of objects that had never been shown in that way before. No painter had ever included a mirror like the one in the center of the Arnolfinis' portrait. It would have been difficult for van Eyck to draw. But anyone who drew one afterward would have his example to follow. That's true of almost everything in the picture: the slightly dirty wooden clogs, the oranges by the window, the chandelier. Once van Eyck had found ways to paint them, other artists could imitate him.

DAVID HOCKNEY *Mr and Mrs Clark and Percy, 1970–71*

DAVID: My picture, painted in 1971, is of my friends Celia Birtwell and Ossie Clark in their flat in Notting Hill Gate in London.

MARTIN: Some pictures appeal to us even if the objects in them become unfamiliar. The white dial telephone in the corner of your picture, rather smart and stylish in 1971, looks rather peculiar to us now (as does Giovanni Arnolfini's strange hat or his wife's green gown). Perhaps even our readers will wonder what on earth the white phone was, but they'll probably still look with pleasure and interest at the two people in the picture, the flowers, and Percy the cat—just as we look at the animals painted on the walls of ancient caves, without knowing who created them or why they did so.

UTAGAWA HIROSHIGE *View of the Harbour (Miya: Station no. 42)*, c. 1847–52

DAVID: Pictures influence other pictures. Vincent van Gogh was one of the first artists in 19th-century Europe to use the bold colors and lines he'd seen in Japanese art. He went to live in Arles in the south of France where the sunlight was strong and bright. Van Gogh's use of intense color influenced a lot of artists later.

VINCENT VAN GOGH *Père Tanguy*, 1887

He took one more thing from Japanese art, too: the absence of shadows. We'll think more about the way artists use light and shadows later in this book.

MARTIN: In this picture of his friend Père Tanguy, van Gogh has used a set of Japanese woodblock prints from his collection as a striking backdrop. In the later 19th century, artists collected these prints with great enthusiasm. They suggested a new way of working. Art didn't have to look like the real world anymore.

DAVID: Going back to van Eyck, and his picture of Arnolfini, I love imagining him at work. His workshop would have been rather like a Hollywood film studio. Wigs, armor, chandeliers, models—all kinds of props. You just have to look at the paintings to see that. It isn't possible to paint like that from imagination. It must have been rather like making a movie: costumes, lighting, camera, let's go!

MARTIN: There are lots of connections between painting, photography, and cinema. We'll talk about them in more detail later in the book.

DAVID: When I was young the cinema was always called the pictures: Can we go to the pictures, Mum? "Movies" are moving pictures, but they are pictures all the same.

MARTIN: Movies were made in Hollywood because of the strong California light. In other words, the makers of film were dealing with a problem that occupied the minds of many great painters, including Caravaggio and Leonardo da Vinci: lighting. They had to work out how to light the subject to make the most powerful picture.

LEONARDO DA VINCI *Mona Lisa, c. 1503–19*   Photograph of Marlene Dietrich, *c.* 1937

DAVID: Leonardo's great painting the *Mona Lisa* is one of the first portraits with very blended shadows. That face is marvelously lit. Look at the shadow under the nose, and that smile, and the way da Vinci blends his colors from the light to the dark flesh. I've no idea how he did it—the paint would have taken a long time to put on. In fact, the way it is lit reminds me of the photographs of the great Hollywood actress Marlene Dietrich.

DAVID: I think Walt Disney was a great American artist. Who were the most famous stars of the 1930s and 1940s? Mickey Mouse and Donald Duck! And they are still around today.

If you look at the film *Pinocchio* frame by frame, you'll see the amazing sequence where Pinocchio goes into the whale's stomach with Geppetto. They light a fire to make the thing belch, then there's a wonderful scene where they are thrown out of the whale. Then the whale comes after them. The raft is on the water and in a storm until they are finally cast up on a beach.

When I noticed how it was done, I was astonished. There are passages that look like Chinese art and Japanese prints, with white sea foam and swirling waves. The Disney animators had obviously looked at these, along with photographs of water. When Pinocchio and Geppetto are dumped on the shore, the water washes up with bubbles in it, then sinks into the sand. It's fantastic.

WALT DISNEY PRODUCTIONS Film still from *Pinocchio*, 1940

UTAGAWA HIROSHIGE Detail from *Naruto Whirlpool, Awa Province, c.* 1853

MARTIN: History does not move forward in straight lines. All artists encounter certain problems—how to use the space to tell stories in a picture, for example, or how to make a brush or pen mark look like a person or thing. So we'll begin this book by looking at some of these ideas before going on to look at particular times and places.

We'll also talk about how technology has affected the history of pictures. Since the invention of the photograph, newspapers, moving pictures, television, the Internet, and the smartphone have made it possible to share billions of pictures at lightning speed, all around the world. Pictures are changing, fast. More people are making them and editing them, more rapidly, than ever before.

DAVID: People like pictures. They have powerful effects on the way we see the world around us. Many people have always preferred looking at pictures to reading; perhaps they always will. I think that humans like images even more than words. I like looking at the world and I've always been interested in how we see, and what we see. The history of pictures begins in the caves and ends, at the moment, with an iPad. Who knows where it will go next?

25

2

MAKING MARKS
What makes an interesting mark?

Carving of a lion, Les Combarelles cave, France, *c.* 12,000 BCE

DAVID: The moment you put down two or three marks on a piece of paper, they will start to look like something. If you draw two little lines they might look like two figures or two trees. If you put down four marks, everyone knows it could be a face. We read all kinds of things into marks. You can suggest landscape, people, or animals with very little.

MARTIN: When we look at the world, we are often able to see one thing as another. Leonardo da Vinci said that when he looked at the random shapes, scratches, and patterns on walls and stones all around him he imagined incredible landscapes, figures, and faces. Look at this picture of a cave lion, which is more than 14,000 years old. Ancient artists carved into the rock with stone tools and turned natural cracks and bulges in the cave wall into an image of a great beast.

DAVID: What makes a mark interesting? I think it's movement—the way an artist uses the pencil or brush. You can often see whether they have made the line very fast or quite slowly.

Chinese painters used to practice by drawing the same images over and over again. Let's say they were drawing a bird. They might start with ten marks, then slowly get it down to three or four. I once watched a young Chinese artist painting cats, placing every mark perfectly. The characters of Chinese writing are closely linked with painting, too. Tiny changes in the marks create entirely new meanings.

WU ZHEN Leaf from an album of bamboo drawings, 1350

MUQI *Six Persimmons*, 13th century

In the 13th century, the Chinese priest and painter Muqi created this delicate picture of six pieces of fruit with ink on silk. He hardly made any marks at all—you can almost count the number of brushstrokes. Yet he still managed to make each piece of fruit look different.

At this time, Chinese artists didn't often use color, so the way they used ink and controlled the brush was especially important. One writer on art in the Ming dynasty counted twenty-six different ways to paint rocks and twenty-seven ways to paint leaves on trees!

DAVID: Artists borrow marks from one another all the time. You can see it when you look closely at their pictures. They learn by copying the work of other artists. I think Rembrandt, who was working in Amsterdam in the 17th century, had probably seen a few Chinese drawings.

Amsterdam was a port and the Dutch were trading a great deal in the Far East. They would have brought pictures back on their ships, along with spices, porcelain, and silk.

Look at Rembrandt's sketch of a child learning to walk. The child is being held by her mother and older sister. The mother grips the child firmly, the sister more hesitantly. There's a hint of worry in the child's face, shown only by one or two faint marks. The father, who crouches on the left, has excited eyes that are two beautiful ink blobs.

REMBRANDT VAN RIJN *A child being taught to walk, c. 1656*

Rembrandt doesn't use many lines! But we can still tell that the mother's skirt is a bit ragged and that the milkmaid's bucket is full and heavy. It's an incredible drawing.

Rembrandt's drawings aren't that big, because paper was very expensive. He had to use every bit of it! When they are reproduced small you don't catch all the details, but if you see them blown up, then look again, you notice more. You see the beauty of the drawing.

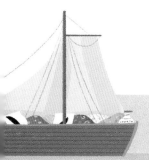

DAVID: At one time, almost everybody could draw. Before photography, drawing was even taught at the U.S. Military Academy because officers in the army had to be able to do it. Engineers needed to be able to draw a machine. It was the same for 30,000 years. Drawing extremely well is something you need to learn.

MARTIN: We know that many famous artists, such as Raphael, Michelangelo, and J. M. W. Turner, began to work in their early teens. It's like playing tennis or a musical instrument—you need to practice every day.

Michelangelo's drawings, like this one of a man running, impressed everyone who met him. A famous story tells of how, in 1496, Jacopo Gallo, a Roman aristocrat, visited the artist's house. He wanted to see some of Michelangelo's art. Michelangelo had no work there to show him, but he was able to take his quill pen and draw a hand so perfectly that Gallo was speechless.

DAVID: You would be astonished to see a Michelangelo drawing appear in front of your eyes, especially if you didn't know much about him. Michelangelo's drawings are amazing. You don't know how he did some of them.

MICHELANGELO *Figure Study of a Running Man*, c. 1527–60

WILLIAM-ADOLPHE BOUGUEREAU *Mignon* (detail), 1869

MARTIN: In the late 18th century, brushstrokes seemed to disappear. The paintings that were shown in exhibitions in large galleries like the Royal Academy in London or the Salon in Paris had smooth surfaces. You couldn't really see any marks at all. In fact, they looked a bit like photographs.

But when Édouard Manet began painting in Paris in the 1850s and 1860s, the brushstroke came back! His pictures—like this one of the artist Berthe Morisot—looked quite different from everyone else's. They were lively and full of energy. After Manet came Claude Monet, the Impressionists, and Vincent van Gogh. At the time people criticized all of them for showing pictures that looked like sketches rather than finished paintings.

ÉDOUARD MANET *Berthe Morisot with a Bouquet of Violets*, 1872

DAVID: Monet and the Impressionists painted out in the open air, rather than working in their studios. They worked in all weather conditions, often at great speed. For example, there are some wonderful Monet paintings of ice melting on the River Seine. It was so rare for there to be ice on the Seine that Monet would have had to go down to the river and paint it straightaway.

MARTIN: The winter of 1879–80 was one of the coldest of the 19th century. The River Seine formed a thick coating of ice, which was covered by deep layers of snow. At the time Monet was living in Vétheuil, a small town just outside Paris. On the night of January 4, we're told, a thaw began to melt the ice, starting in the east and spreading west on the Seine.

DAVID: As soon as Monet heard that there were ice floes in the Seine, he must have set to work. The ice might not have lasted even a night once the thaw had begun. That would have made him work very fast. When the sun is setting, you know that you only have one hour before the light goes, so you work faster. He must have been doing very intense looking! Pictures can make us see things that we might not notice without them. Monet made us see the world a bit more clearly.

CLAUDE MONET *Breakup of the Ice,* 1880

DAVID: I noticed how quickly the light and the sky changed in Yorkshire when I was painting there. It has a very similar climate to northern France, where Monet was working. In the charcoal landscapes I drew in Woldgate, East Yorkshire, during the spring of 2013, I used a big range of marks. You have to have a variety. I'd looked at Pablo Picasso, Henri Matisse, and Raoul Dufy. But I only made the marks a stick of charcoal can make; that's all you can do.

There's a history of marks as well as a history of pictures! You can look at the different kind of marks that artists use and borrow from one another—the marks they make with pen, charcoal, pencil, as well as the strokes they make with the brush and paint. And you'll see them even more clearly by learning to draw and copying them yourself.

RAOUL DUFY *The Avenue du Bois de Boulogne*, 1928

DAVID HOCKNEY *Woldgate, 26 May, 2013*, 2013

LIGHT AND SHADOWS
What is a shadow exactly?

MARTIN: Nearly 2,000 years ago, the Roman author Pliny the Elder wrote that the ancient Egyptians and Greeks both claimed they invented the idea of portrait painting. They made their pictures by tracing around shadows of the human figure.

But we now know that painting was at least 30,000 years old when Pliny was writing. Early artists traced outlines and shadows, too. Deep in the caves of southern France, Spain, Argentina, and at other prehistoric sites, we can still see images that were made by blowing paint made of earth or clay around the artist's hand, rather like stencils. In a way, they were the first signed pictures.

Much later, in 18th- and 19th-century Europe, "silhouettes" were a cheap and popular type of portrait. They were also known as "shades" or "profiles." To make them, artists used peculiar contraptions like the one in the picture opposite.

Hand silhouettes in the *Cueva de las Manos* or Cave of Hands, Santa Cruz, Argentina, *c.* 7000–1000 BCE

THOMAS HOLLOWAY *A Sure and Convenient Machine for Drawing Silhouettes*, 1792

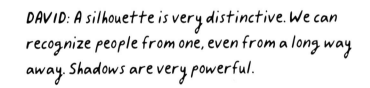

DAVID: A silhouette is very distinctive. We can recognize people from one, even from a long way away. Shadows are very powerful.

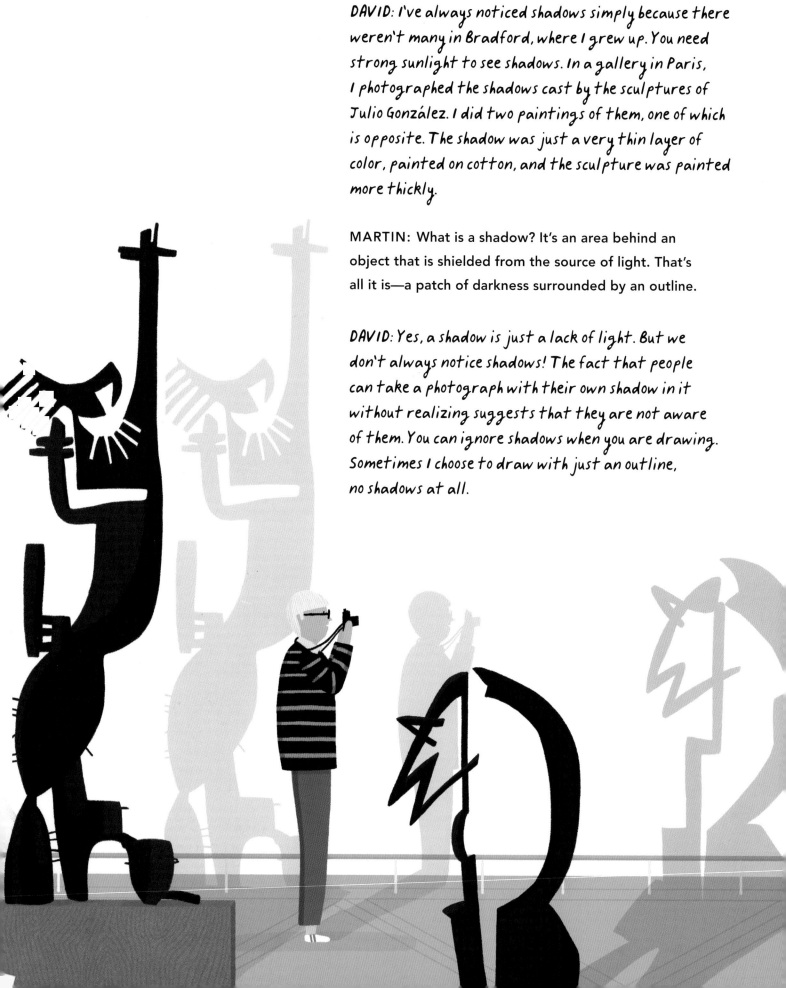

DAVID: I've always noticed shadows simply because there weren't many in Bradford, where I grew up. You need strong sunlight to see shadows. In a gallery in Paris, I photographed the shadows cast by the sculptures of Julio González. I did two paintings of them, one of which is opposite. The shadow was just a very thin layer of color, painted on cotton, and the sculpture was painted more thickly.

MARTIN: What is a shadow? It's an area behind an object that is shielded from the source of light. That's all it is—a patch of darkness surrounded by an outline.

DAVID: Yes, a shadow is just a lack of light. But we don't always notice shadows! The fact that people can take a photograph with their own shadow in it without realizing suggests that they are not aware of them. You can ignore shadows when you are drawing. Sometimes I choose to draw with just an outline, no shadows at all.

DAVID HOCKNEY *Gonzalez and Shadow*, 1971

MARTIN: Shadows can trick us. They are not the thing itself. In the classic film *The Third Man* from 1949, the shadow of the hero/villain Harry Lime is seen disappearing down a street in Vienna. In fact, Orson Welles, the actor playing Lime, wasn't on set that day, so the shadow is actually that of the assistant director, wearing an oversized overcoat and padding.

Shadows don't just give us information; they also create illusions. Artists Tim Noble and Sue Webster have made a set of sculptures that at first glance look just like a pile of scrap metal. But look at the surprising shadows they throw on the wall! They cast incredibly accurate human figures. The picture on the right is actually a shadow self-portrait.

Opposite: TIM NOBLE and SUE WEBSTER *HE/SHE* (detail), 2004

DAVID: How do artists make objects look as if they are right in front of us? To see an object in three dimensions you need light and shadows.

MARTIN: There's a wonderful story of a competition between two ancient Greek artists, Zeuxis and Parrhasios. They wanted to decide who could paint a better picture. Zeuxis painted a bunch of grapes so successfully that birds fluttered around, attracted to the fruit. But, just as he was congratulating himself on his victory, he noticed that Parrhasios's picture was still covered by a piece of cloth. When he asked for the fabric to be removed, it turned out that the cloth was part of the painting. Parrhasios's picture was a trick—but he certainly won the competition! Of course, we don't know what either artist's picture would have looked like. Perhaps they might have looked a little like this wall painting from the house of Julia Felix at Pompeii, which was created around the time of the story.

Still Life with Bowls of Fruit and Wine Jar, c. 70 CE

CLARA PEETERS *Still Life with Fruit, Dead Birds, and a Monkey*, date unknown

DAVID: By the 16th and 17th centuries, artists across Europe were producing thousands of "still life" paintings. They set up arrangements of baskets of fruit or vases of flowers in strong light and painted them with deep, dark shadows. In a way, like the artists in the story of the birds pecking at the painting of grapes, they were competing to produce more and more convincing images. How did they do it?

DAVID: The first painter to use strong light and shadows in this way was the Italian painter Caravaggio, who became famous while he was working in Rome in the late 16th century. I've looked at his pictures over and over again. He worked out how to light things dramatically. His shadows are so dark! You don't find shadows like that in nature.

For many years, I've been thinking about how Caravaggio—and other artists—could have made their pictures look so real. I think Caravaggio made his pictures by projecting images of the models posing in his studio straight onto his canvas.

He would have set them up in a brightly lit space, probably next to a window, while he worked in a dark area behind a wall or screen. The image would have been projected through a tiny hole in the wall—perfect, but upside down! When I tried it for myself, the results were spectacular.

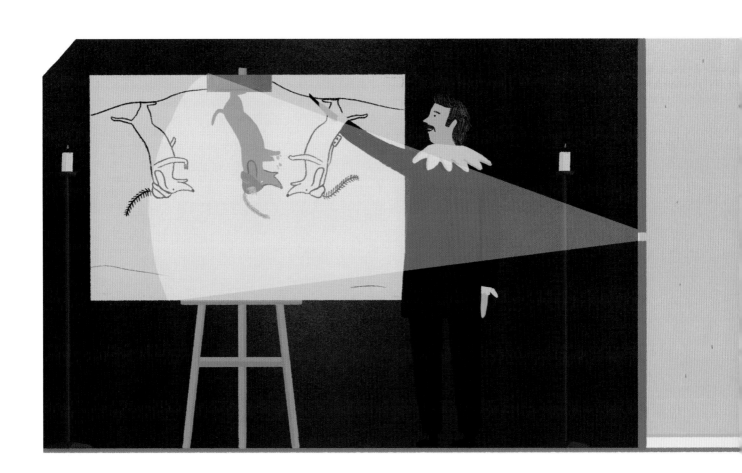

CARAVAGGIO *The Taking of Christ, c. 1602*

By projecting first this figure, then that figure—or part of a figure, an arm or a face—Caravaggio could slowly make his picture. He would have had to work very quickly to draw the outline of his models before they moved or took a break. It would have been hard work!

MARTIN: The same people appear in many of Caravaggio's pictures. There's a man with a growth on his nostril, walrus mustache, and grizzled hair who turns up in at least three paintings from around the same time. He is the man on the right in *The Supper at Emmaus*. Look closely, and you'll spot the same wrinkle-browed fellow twice in *The Incredulity of St. Thomas*. As well as playing the disciple standing in the background, he is also posing as the figure of St. Thomas at the front (although Caravaggio has given him some hair).

DAVID: Caravaggio had an enormous influence on later artists. His style spread across Europe, and soon many other artists were painting scenes with dramatic lighting. Next time you're looking at pictures, think about the way the artist has used light—and look at the shadows.

CARAVAGGIO *The Supper at Emmaus*, 1601

CARAVAGGIO *The Incredulity of St. Thomas, 1601–02*

Details from Caravaggio's paintings show the same model appearing three times.

4

WATCH THIS SPACE
How do artists set the scene?

DAVID: When I begin a picture, one of the first questions I have to ask is: What do I do with the space? How can I tell a story in this space? A big thing in drawing is being able to put a figure in space.

When we look at a scene, we ask: What do I see first? What do I see second? What do I see third? A photograph sees it all at once—in one click of the lens from a single point of view—but we don't. We need time to take it all in. Our eyes are always moving.

DAVID HOCKNEY *The Second Marriage*, 1963

1

ANDREI RUBLEV *Holy Trinity (Troitsa)*, 1425–27

3

MARTIN: The art of arranging objects in space on a flat surface, and making them look as if they have depth and distance, is called "perspective." Medieval paintings of an altar, table, or throne, like this one by Andrei Rublev, would often show both left and right sides of an object at once.

MARTIN: During the early 15th century in the Italian city of Florence, artists began to make pictures that showed space in a new way. They imagined lines disappearing toward a point in the distance, the way a straight road or railway track does if you look along it. The artist could work out exactly how big or small any person or thing along the lines should be.

The result was a picture that looked similar to how a camera lens sees the world, or a person does, if they keep very still with one eye closed. Anything up close was large, but along the lines things appeared to get smaller and smaller until finally they disappeared into the distance. You can see this in many paintings from the time, as in Paolo Uccello's *The Hunt in the Forest*.

PAOLO UCCELLO *The Hunt in the Forest* (detail), *c.* 1470

DAVID: Not all artists worked this way. In the pictures of Jan van Eyck, who was working in northern Europe, you always feel you are close to everything, even the distant faces in the crowd.

In the Canon van der Paele altarpiece, van Eyck's figures are on a quite different scale from the church in which they are set, but it takes some time to notice that—if you ever do.

They are close up, right in front of you; it's as if you are there, too. You might say the figures are too big for the architecture. At the time, people would have seen the picture as amazingly real, which it still is. Look at the gold thread on the bishop's coat, and the way the armor gleams. It's so rich in detail.

JAN VAN EYCK *The Madonna with Canon van der Paele*, 1436

DAVID HOCKNEY *Pearblossom Hwy., 11–18 April 1986 (second version)*, 1986

DAVID: In the 1980s I started making pictures that explored all these ideas about perspective. My picture of Pearblossom Highway in California is a collage of hundreds of photographs all stuck together. It looks as if it has been taken from one spot—looking straight down the road—but that's not the case! I wanted to show that humans don't see the world from one point of view; our eyes move around all the time, and we move, too. So I moved about the landscape, taking every photograph from a different place. I wanted to get right up close to my subjects and capture the gravelly surface of the road, the desert plants and grasses, the cans and bottles on the ground.

I climbed up a ladder to photograph the road sign and the cactus. The markings on the road were also done from a ladder— you had to be up above them, looking straight down.

It took a week to do the pictures. I worked from about 9:00 to 11:00 every morning, because I needed the sun in the same place each day. There are around 850 photographs in the final picture!

WANG HUI *Kangxi Emperor's Southern Inspection Tour* (detail), 1689

DAVID: In Chinese and Japanese painting, your eyes wander around the picture. It's as if you are taking a journey through the landscape, moving right through it. You don't stop in one place—you just keep going.

MARTIN: Chinese landscape artists created epic, impressive works. Wang Hui created a set of twelve silk handscrolls for the Kangxi emperor to record the emperor's journey across southern China. The detail opposite—of villagers crossing the Grand Canal—is just one small part of a much bigger picture. Other scrolls in the series show great mountain peaks and jagged hills towering toward the sky.

DAVID: The Chinese handscroll is a different sort of picture. Unlike a painting you might see hanging on the wall of a gallery, the scroll is kept in a box, only to be looked at on special occasions. You can't see the whole image all at once. You have to look at it one section at a time, so it doesn't really have edges in a normal sense. I own a copy of a 13th-century scroll (pictured below)—you can see the way you have to unroll it to look at the landscape.

Copy of HUANG KUNG-WANG *Dwelling in the Fu-ch'un Mountains*, 1347

LEONARDO DA VINCI *The Last Supper*, 1494–99

MARTIN: Artists tell stories in pictures. Every part of Leonardo da Vinci's *The Last Supper* was designed to draw the viewer into the drama. It shows Jesus Christ having a meal with his disciples. Leonardo has painted the moment in the story when Christ tells the group that one of them is going to betray him and therefore send him to his death. He painted it on the end wall of an actual dining hall in a monastery in Milan. Looking at the background, we can see that he has used perspective to extend the space and make it look as if the group is actually sitting in the room.

This is always a great challenge for artists: how to tell a story that unfolds through time in a single image. Edward Hopper's *Nighthawks* looks rather like a film still—we can imagine what has just happened to the characters in the picture, and what might happen next.

There are other ways of telling stories in pictures, of course. Events from different times might be shown side by side in the same space. Or artists might show a sequence of dramatic episodes one after another, like in a comic book.

EDWARD HOPPER *Nighthawks*, 1942

JUAN GRIS *The Violin*, 1916

MARTIN: In the early 20th century, Pablo Picasso and Georges Braque found a totally new way of painting space. Their style became known as Cubism. Look at this picture of a violin by the Cubist artist Juan Gris. Instead of painting the violin from one point of view, he has included many angles and views, all at once.

DAVID: Cubism was an attack on the perspective that artists had used for 500 years. It was the first big, big change. Most Cubist paintings are of something very close to us: a collection of objects on a table, or a person sitting on a chair. They didn't paint buildings or architecture.

In Picasso's pictures, you can often see the front and back of a person at the same time. That means you've walked around them. I like to think of it as a sort of memory picture and a moving picture, too. The kind of picture we might make in our heads.

MIRRORS AND REFLECTIONS
How do artists play with light?

DAVID: Mirrors are very powerful things because they can make pictures. Your own pictures look different in a mirror, and a mirror can make the real world look like a picture. Leonardo da Vinci suggested painters should judge their works by looking at them in a flat mirror. It's a good way of looking at things from another point of view.

MARTIN: Humans have been interested in mirrors since ancient times. In fact, mirrors are almost as old as pictures. Polished stone mirrors some six thousand years old have been discovered in Anatolia, Turkey. The ancient Greeks had mirrors made of polished bronze and other metals. So it's no surprise that there are pictures of reflections in ancient art.

Look at the shining shield in the picture opposite, which shows a battle between Alexander the Great and the Persian king Darius. The huge disc, possibly made of polished silver, is falling to the ground. A soldier raises his hand in an effort to prevent the thing crashing on him. His sad face is reflected in the shield.

ERETRIA PAINTER *Seated woman holding a mirror*, 430 BCE
Opposite: *The Battle of Issus between Alexander the Great and Darius* (detail), *c.* 315 BCE

MARTIN: Many painters wanted to make pictures as similar to mirror images as possible. The Italian artist Parmigianino even had a special curved piece of wood made so that his picture would look just like what he saw when he looked in the mirror. He then painted exactly what he saw there: at the bottom of the picture, his hand is even bigger than his face; at the top, the walls curve all around him.

PARMIGIANINO *Self-Portrait in a Convex Mirror*, 1523–24

RENÉ MAGRITTE *Not to be reproduced*, 1937

A mirror seems to show us truth but, of course, it doesn't really. The image is reversed and flattened, and can be changed by the curve or color of the reflecting surface. A mirror image is at once true and a lie!

René Magritte's painting *Not to be reproduced* plays with this idea. Look at the "reflection" of the suited gentleman in the mirror. It's impossible, of course.

DIEGO VELÁZQUEZ *Las Meninas, c.* 1656

MARTIN: *Las Meninas,* by the Spanish artist Diego Velázquez, is one of the most celebrated paintings in European art. Among many other things, it's a picture about a reflection.

DIEGO VELÁZQUEZ *Las Meninas* (detail), *c.* 1656

In the center of the picture we can see the five-year-old Spanish princess Margarita Teresa surrounded by the people who lived with her in the royal palace (*las meninas* means "the maids"). Velázquez has included himself in the picture, too—he's there at the front working on a huge canvas, with his palette and paintbrush in hand.

Toward the back of the picture is another mirror that shows a reflection of the king, Philip IV, and his queen. Some people think it's a reflection of the picture on which Velázquez is working, in which case *Las Meninas* is a picture of a reflection of a picture!

Originally, Velázquez—who lived in the palace—made the painting to hang in King Philip's private apartments. So when the king looked at it, he didn't just see his royal painter looking at him. He also saw an image of himself in a mirror, looking back.

MARTIN: *Las Meninas* is set in a real place: a long, high room in the prince's quarters in the Royal Alcázar Palace in Madrid. The light in the picture is spectacular. Look at how it catches the side of the canvas, the princess's gleaming hair, and the glittering embroidery on everyone's clothes. If you look at the picture up close, you can see the flickering marks Velázquez made with his brush.

DAVID: Highlights are a great way of adding more information to pictures. When I started drawing on the iPhone and iPad, where the image itself was glowing, I was attracted to subjects that shine and catch reflections—such as vases with water in them or a gleaming silver fruit dish.

Look at the surface of the fruit dish in the picture opposite; you can see the surroundings, as if in a curved mirror. There are also highlights, which are reflections so bright you don't see the image, just the sparkling brilliance. There are highlights on the apples as well, but duller ones because their skins are less shiny.

DAVID HOCKNEY *Untitled, 24 February 2011, 2011*

MARTIN: Just like shadows, we find reflections in nature. From the earliest times, people must have been aware of them in still and moving water and they remain a popular subject for pictures. Of course, reflections are pictures, in a way.

Claude Monet made many pictures of reflections. In his great water lily paintings, which he created in his incredible garden at Giverny, just outside Paris, the surface of the painting, the water, and the reflections of sky and trees seem to merge into one.

DAVID: Monet spent years creating his garden at Giverny. It was a lot of work. The water for the lily ponds had to be still, not running, for example, to create the reflections he wanted. It was a fantastic thing to do. Monet was almost sixty when he began these pictures of water lilies; he carried on painting them right up until he died at the age of eighty-six.

CLAUDE MONET *Nymphéas*, 1905

DAVID HOCKNEY *Study of Water, Phoenix, Arizona, 1976*

Painting water is a great challenge—but it's a nice problem! By the sea you get a special light, because of the reflections. It's clear and sharp. I started painting pictures of swimming pools in California when I moved there in the 1960s. The swimming pool, unlike the pond, reflects light. Those dancing lines I used to paint on the pools are really on the surface of the water. I liked to think of it as a kind of rippling, moving mirror.

6

PAINTING AND PHOTOGRAPHY
What tools do artists use?

DAVID: Photography was invented in 1839, but artists had been working in a way that I'd call "photographic" for several centuries before then. Paintings and photographs have a lot in common.

MARTIN: Let's look at *The Little Street* by Johannes Vermeer. It is an extraordinary picture. He painted it around 1658. You really believe that a color photograph of a 17th-century Dutch town would look much like this. The cobbled street, crumbling bricks, and worn white paint of the walls are all recorded with incredible detail.

DAVID: Vermeer lived and worked in the city of Delft. This scene may have been the view from his window. Nobody really knows how Vermeer made his paintings. It can't be entirely explained, although many different ideas have been suggested. We've talked about the way Caravaggio might have projected images onto his canvas. I think Vermeer worked in a similar way. But he used a powerful lens that could pick up a lot of detail.

MARTIN: The Netherlands was a center of lens making. The earliest telescopes were invented there in 1608. In fact, Vermeer lived only streets away from some of the few people in Europe who could make high-quality lenses.

DAVID: Artists often kept their working methods secret. They didn't want everyone to know how they made their pictures! Perhaps they thought people would think less of them. But the tools artists use don't make marks; they don't make the painting. Vermeer probably used the same equipment as many other artists. He just painted his pictures better.

JOHANNES VERMEER *The Little Street, c.* 1658

WENCESLAUS HOLLAR *A View from St. Mary's, Southwark, Looking Toward Westminster* (detail), *c.* 1638

MARTIN: In the 17th and 18th centuries, various tools for creating pictures were developed and widely used by artists. One called the "camera obscura" was small enough to be carried around and used outdoors. Instead of working behind a screen in the studio the way I think Caravaggio did, artists could now draw lifelike pictures in the open air. With this portable "camera"—which had a lens set into the side of the box—artists could project images onto their paper or canvas.

This picture by Wenceslaus Hollar is a good example of a "camera drawing." Using the projection, Hollar would have been able to trace the outline of the houses quickly and precisely. Look at the way he's used loose, looping lines for the leaves of the trees.

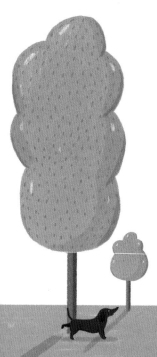

DAVID: In 1807, the scientist William Hyde Wollaston created a rival to the camera obscura, which he called the "camera lucida." This was a glass prism mounted on a brass rod. By looking through the glass at a certain angle, it was possible to see a projection of the subject on the drawing paper.

JEAN-AUGUSTE-DOMINIQUE INGRES *Portrait of Madame Louis-François Godinot (detail)*, 1829

DAVID: When I went to an exhibition of work by the French painter Jean-Auguste-Dominique Ingres at the National Gallery in London, I was struck by his beautiful portrait drawings. The features were incredibly accurate, but the pictures themselves were so small. What made them even more astonishing was that the sitters were all strangers (it's much easier to catch the likeness of someone you know well). Ingres had completed most of them in a single day. How had he done it, I asked myself.

It's my view that Ingres made these portraits—like this one of Madame Godinot—with the camera lucida that Wollaston invented. The lines of her dress are the biggest

DAVID HOCKNEY *Maria Vasquez. London. 21 December 1999* (detail), 1999

clue. You can see that they have been drawn quickly; it's as if they have been traced.

I decided to try using a camera lucida myself. I drew hundreds of portraits with it, including a whole series of pictures of National Gallery guards. It actually is very tricky to use—if you move your eye, the image on the page is lost. You must work quickly and learn to mark the key points of your subject's features.

Making a drawing from a projected image involves thought and choice in the same way as making any other kind of line. There are always decisions about what kind of marks to make.

MARTIN: In the 19th century, artists and scientists searched for a way of "fixing" the pictures that they saw in their camera obscuras. This is how photography was invented—by several people, all at the same time.

DAVID: Early photographers and artists had a lot in common. They were using similar equipment! In the 1830s, the British inventor William Henry Fox Talbot found a way to make the picture permanent. His friend John Herschel gave him a recipe for chemicals that fixed pictures onto a special kind of paper. This was an important discovery. It meant that Fox Talbot's pictures could be printed more than once. At the same time, over in Paris, a painter called Louis Daguerre had invented another way of making camera pictures. He used chemicals that fixed the image permanently onto metal plates.

WILLIAM HENRY FOX TALBOT William Henry Fox Talbot (right) with assistants and camera obscura, 1846

JULIA MARGARET CAMERON *Sir John Herschel*, 1867

MARTIN: Early cameras were big and bulky, and sitters had to be incredibly patient. Julia Margaret Cameron needed her subjects to stay completely still for as long as four minutes while she took the picture. She worked in low light, and some parts of her pictures are deliberately blurred or out of focus—but they have a great atmosphere.

ANDRÉ-ADOLPHE-EUGÈNE DISDÉRI *Prince Richard de Metternich and Princess Pauline de Metternich, 1860*

DAVID: Many of the best early photographs are portraits; some have hardly been bettered in a hundred and forty years. It's no surprise that painters, like the French artist Edgar Degas, were fascinated with photography. Degas was a good photographer himself.

MARTIN: Degas sometimes based paintings on photographs, as he did in the case of this portrait of Princess Pauline de Metternich. His picture, rather strangely, looks more like a photograph than a painting. Degas added the "blur" you would find in an out-of-focus photo, or one in which the subject has moved.

DAVID: Photography also affected the way people saw the art of the past. Prints of famous works already existed, but from 1850 onward it became possible to photograph paintings. Before photography, it would have been difficult to see and remember all the pictures that had been made in separate places all over the world.

EDGAR DEGAS *Princess Pauline de Metternich, c. 1865*

But once photographs existed all that changed. Now, with the Internet, we have literally billions of pictures at our fingertips. There's almost no picture we can't find.

DAVID: In the early days of photography, only rich people could take their own photographs. And until recently, using a camera still needed great skill—it was difficult to get the focus and lighting just right. Now with digital cameras, pictures are almost perfect each time. Everyone is a photographer!

MARTIN: The first cameras were heavy. It took two people to carry the camera Julia Margaret Cameron used in the 1860s. In 1888 Kodak made the first portable box camera. That meant passing moments of everyday life—holidays, parties—could be transformed into pictures and put in a photo album. It was a completely new way of remembering events. The painter Maurice Denis took this photograph of two women swinging his daughter Madeleine between them on the beach in Brittany. This was the kind of moment that millions of people were now able to capture.

MAURICE DENIS *Two girls, wading in the sea, swinging little Madeleine, Perros-Guirec, 1909*

HENRI CARTIER-BRESSON *Place de l'Europe.*
Gare Saint Lazare, 1932

DAVID: Photography changed again when a high-quality, lightweight, handheld camera called the Leica was launched in 1925.

MARTIN: Street photographers such as Henri Cartier-Bresson and Robert Frank used the Leica. It was a camera that enabled someone with the necessary skills to take a picture of just about anything, anywhere. But the photographer had to be prepared to shoot at almost any moment. "You have to be quick to take something," as Robert Frank put it. "The world changes all the time and it doesn't come back. You have to be ready."

HANNAH HÖCH *Cut with the Kitchen Knife* (detail), 1919–20

MARTIN: In the 1930s artists like Hannah Höch created pictures called "collages" by cutting up and rearranging dozens of photographs, and pieces of text, from newspapers and magazines.

Piecing together different photographic images to make a new picture was a technique that had been used since the earliest days of photography. Early photographers wanted to echo the way that painters created their pictures by combining many figures and views.

DAVID: Artists still work that way today! In my photograph that you can see below, every figure, face, and chair was photographed separately. If you look closely, you can see that some of the people in the picture appear more than once. I edited the photographs and combined them on a computer. I had to look at every element in the picture really carefully and decide where to put it.

This is exactly what Caravaggio was doing in 1600 and what some early photographers were doing in 1860 who stuck bits of different prints together to make one picture. The techniques are old! It's just the tools that are new.

DAVID HOCKNEY *4 Blue Stools*, 2014

7

MOVING PICTURES
Can pictures really move?

MARTIN: Over the centuries, people invented many ways of tricking the human eye into thinking images were moving. The zoetrope—a drum of spinning images—and the flick book still entertain us today. The science actually is quite simple. If the eye sees more than sixteen images per second it will join them into one "moving picture." Of course, it is an illusion. Strictly speaking, there is no such thing as a moving picture, only a series of still ones.

In 1878 Eadweard Muybridge devised a way of photographing a horse in rapid motion. He set up a racetrack with thread laid across it that triggered the shutters of a series of cameras lined along the course. Muybridge's images of horses and people were not yet quite moving pictures, but looking back at them now, we can see the beginnings of film.

DAVID: Muybridge had a system of a lot of cameras clicking as the horse moved along. But as soon as a camera was invented that could follow the horse, his experiments ended. They led into film. In a way, he was doing little dramas that last a couple of seconds; film just took it over.

MARTIN: In France, Étienne-Jules Marey was also experimenting with photographing movement. His photographs showed multiple movements in the same picture. This new information about how humans and animals move, too fast to be visible to the human eye, was of great interest to some artists.

EADWEARD MUYBRIDGE *The Horse in Motion*, 1878

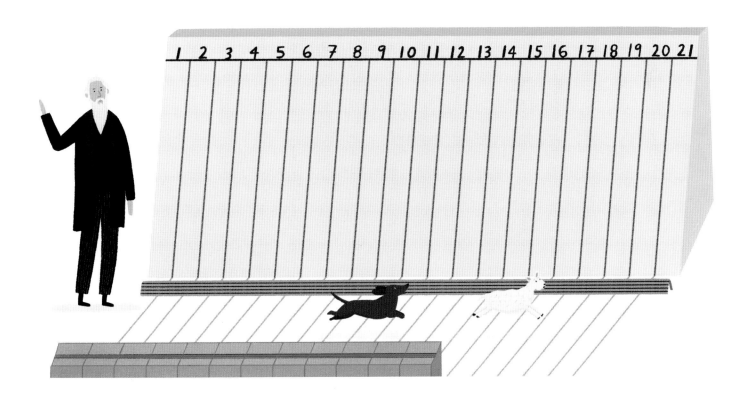

MARTIN: The first public film show was presented by the Lumière brothers in Paris, on December 28, 1895. It included the first film they ever made, a forty-six-second sequence of workers coming out of the gates of the Lumière factory in Lyon. It wasn't particularly interesting—the fact that the picture moved was entertaining enough!

It was another French filmmaker, Georges Méliès, who transformed moving pictures from simply a picture that moved into an imaginative performance. Méliès's masterpiece was *A Trip to the Moon* made in 1902—sixty-seven years before the first moon landing. Early film cameras couldn't move or follow the actors around, so it was really a filmed play, shot scene by scene. This fantastical voyage into space was shot in a studio he'd built himself, full of elaborate costumes, props, and special effects. Each frame was colored in by hand, as was common in the early days of film.

GEORGES MÉLIÈS *A Trip to the Moon*, 1902

WALT DISNEY PRODUCTIONS Film still from *The Jungle Book*, 1967

DAVID: Drawing has always been part of the history of moving pictures. You can understand more about how an elephant walks from looking at the Disney animation *The Jungle Book* than you could from a photograph. It's because the artists who drew that sequence had looked closely at the way the animals' muscles and bones moved, and they made it very clear.

DAVID: Movement is essential in films! That's what you are being asked to look at, and you take it in without thinking. Before films had sound, they relied on movement because it's partly what keeps you glued to the screen. In silent movies, there was a great deal of eye movement. The eyes were outlined with makeup. Actors like Charlie Chaplin (pictured opposite) were always looking this way and that way—speaking with the eyes—and making exaggerated gestures. Once movies with sound arrived, movement diminished. The actors had to stay near the microphone for the sound to be recorded. Once you know that, some scenes can be rather funny!

Charlie Chaplin, still from *City Lights*, 1931

VICTOR FLEMING *The Wizard of Oz*, 1939

MARTIN: Technicolor film came in around 1938. *The Wizard of Oz* from 1939 opens in black-and-white, in Kansas; after the tornado, Dorothy and Toto wake up in Oz and find themselves in full color. Audiences were thrilled! In Technicolor, the red was incredibly bright—that's why Dorothy's slippers are ruby instead of gray like they are in the book.

Ways of filming moving pictures continued to evolve rapidly in the 20th century, and each change suggested new ways of telling stories. Nowadays, we can watch films in 3D, and special effects can be even more dazzling. In one big, obvious fashion the moving picture is different from all others: it moves. But it is still a type of picture.

DAVID: We can find moving pictures in art galleries, too; they hang on the wall next to paintings. They don't have to tell stories, though. And we can decide how much time we spend in front of them. I filmed the Woldgate Woods in East Yorkshire and created a series of moving pictures called *The Four Seasons*. You can sit, surrounded by them on all sides, looking at the wood in spring, summer, autumn, and winter.

There is an important distinction between a still picture and a movie: you bring your time to the painting; the film imposes its time on you. If somebody said, "Come home and watch the world's greatest movie," you might say, "Another day," because it's going to take up a considerable amount of your time. A painting doesn't do that.

DAVID HOCKNEY *The Four Seasons, Woldgate Woods*
(Spring 2011, Summer 2010, Autumn 2010, Winter 2010), 2010–11

8

THE STORY GOES ON
What's next for pictures?

USTWO GAMES *Monument Valley*, 2014

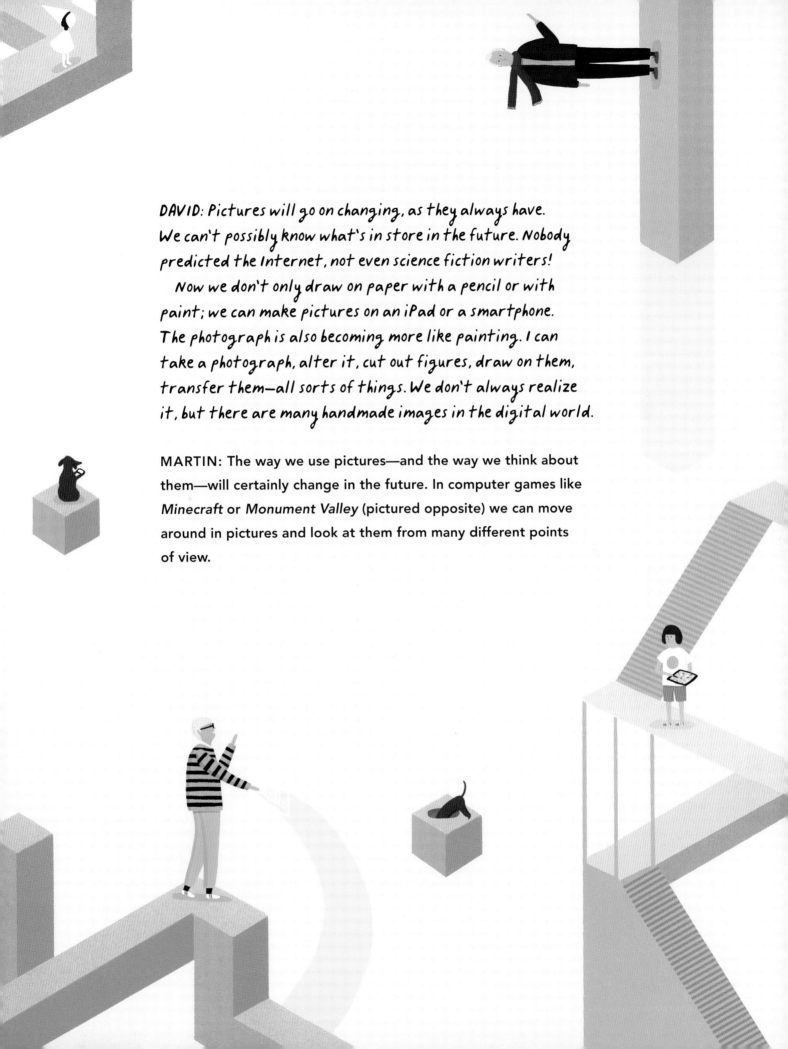

DAVID: Pictures will go on changing, as they always have. We can't possibly know what's in store in the future. Nobody predicted the Internet, not even science fiction writers!

Now we don't only draw on paper with a pencil or with paint; we can make pictures on an iPad or a smartphone. The photograph is also becoming more like painting. I can take a photograph, alter it, cut out figures, draw on them, transfer them—all sorts of things. We don't always realize it, but there are many handmade images in the digital world.

MARTIN: The way we use pictures—and the way we think about them—will certainly change in the future. In computer games like *Minecraft* or *Monument Valley* (pictured opposite) we can move around in pictures and look at them from many different points of view.

MARTIN: Can we believe in pictures? It's a question that comes up again and again. People worried that Caravaggio used real people as models for sacred figures. Early photographers who manipulated their pictures were suspected of being frauds.

DAVID: There's a famous photograph of bombed-out London the morning after an air raid. It's a shot of a milkman walking over the ruins. It was made in 1940 to tell people not to panic—to "Keep calm and carry on." But the man in the picture wasn't a milkman—he was the photographer's assistant; he'd just put on a coat. You could say it was faked, but at the time it had a message to communicate: it was saying "Carry on." If it were a painting, you wouldn't worry about whether a real milkman was the model.

MARTIN: These days it's not unusual to see "fake" photographs of political events or celebrities on the Internet. But people still expect that pictures should tell the truth, and show the world exactly as it is. Perhaps some do so more than others, but none do so completely—because that is impossible.

FRED MORLEY *The London Milkman*, 1940

DAVID: Journalist photographers can still be fired for making collages of different shots. A newspaper photographer is supposed to be a kind of reporter and present the truth of what he or she sees. But you can't always believe what you see, can you? There is no reason why you should believe any more in a photograph than you do in a painting.

DAVID: In the 21st century, smartphones—which so many of us carry around in our pockets—have become completely amazing. We can use them to look at pictures; we can do more with those pictures than ever before.

MARTIN: Pictures have moved from the cave wall, to the temple, the church, the photograph album, the cinema, television, and the computer screen. Many ways of making pictures have been devised, beginning with applying pigment with a stick or a finger, and ending, for now, with computer drawing.

Today, enormous numbers of people are able to take a picture—still or moving—and almost immediately publish it to the world, or at least to their followers and contacts, on apps like Twitter, Instagram, WhatsApp, or Snapchat. The addition of a selfie button to smartphones has transformed pictures just as portable cameras did in the late 19th century. When you take a selfie, you start to see your surroundings as a certain kind of picture, whether you are posing with a friend or celebrity, or in a gallery in front of the *Mona Lisa*. Hundreds of millions of selfies are taken and sent each day!

DAVID: The world today is full of images. But the more photographs you take, the less time you'll spend looking at each one. At one time, there were only a few pictures around; now there are ever-increasing billions each year. What will happen to them all? Probably most of them will be lost. Some people will save things, and it's those that will last.

MARTIN: The history of pictures is all about the images that have happened to survive. Which they will be in the future is impossible to say, but it is likely that they will have some of the qualities we have noticed in these pages. They will be memorable.

DAVID: Some things never change. Some pictures last. People are like pictures—they won't go away.

TIMELINE OF INVENTIONS

BCE stands for "Before the Common Era"
CE stands for "Common Era"

It is thought Jesus was born in the year zero, at the start of the Common Era. Events that occurred before his birth are counted back from the year zero, and events after his birth are counted forward. When it is obvious a date is in the Common Era, the letters CE are not used.

AROUND 30,000 YEARS AGO

Stone tools and natural pigments are used for carving and creating pictures on the walls of caves.

AROUND 1550 BCE

Greek artists paint "fresco" pictures on the walls of tombs and temples working directly in the wet plaster. (Ancient Egyptians used the "dry fresco" method.)

AROUND 200 BCE

Paintbrushes are used in China for calligraphy. They are usually made from bamboo and animal hair.

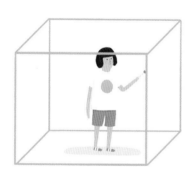

AROUND 1413

Artists in Italy construct a set of rules for painters wanting to create the illusion of space and depth on a flat surface. This is called "perspective."

AROUND 1430

Lenses and mirrors become more widely available and artists begin to use them to view their work.

1439

The printing press is invented by Gutenberg in Germany. Paper is made in large quantities, and gets cheaper so artists can use more of it!

AROUND 100 BCE

Paper is invented in China. By 1085 we begin to find paper mills in Europe. Early paper is rare and expensive.

200 CE

Woodblock printing is invented in China as a way of printing—first, on silk or cloth, and, much later, on paper.

AROUND 1400

By mixing pigments with oil, artists in the Netherlands begin to blend and layer paints to create pictures with smooth surfaces and sharp details.

AROUND 1450

Using different methods of engraving, artists can make many copies of their pictures; we call these "prints."

AROUND 1500

In Venice, Italy, artists start to paint on canvas fabric stretched tight across a wooden frame rather than on wood panels.

AROUND 1600

Tools, like the camera obscura, used to project images onto paper or canvas, become popular.

1780

The first ready-made watercolor paints are sold in London; before, artists had to grind and mix their own pigments.

1839

Photography is invented. Using special chemicals, images can be fixed on paper and reproduced many times. Early cameras are big and heavy.

1841

Portable metal paint tubes are invented; now, artists can paint in oils outdoors in all weather conditions.

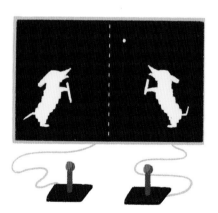

FROM 1960

Acrylic paint becomes a popular tool for artists. It dries quickly, giving bold, flat colors.

FROM 1970

Video games are invented. They present new ways of "playing" with pictures.

FROM 1975

Home computers change the way people use images. Eventually, with photo editing software, pictures can be combined and transformed.

FROM 1888

Small, portable cameras become popular. They are easy to carry around. In 1907 the color photograph is invented.

FROM 1890

The beginnings of cinema. At first, films are silent and in black-and-white; later, they have sound and color.

FROM 1950

Televisions can be found in homes across the world; pictures are sent to many people's TV sets at the same time.

FROM 1989

The Internet makes millions of pictures available to everyone with the click of a button.

FROM 2000

Smartphones and tablets are used by many people across the world for taking photographs and posting pictures online.

ANIMATION a way of making still pictures look as if they are moving by showing a sequence of images very quickly, one after another. A cartoon, a flick book, and a zoetrope are all types of *animation*.

BOX CAMERA an early camera, shaped like a box, containing a *lens* and loaded with a *roll of film* (see p. 96).

CAMERA LUCIDA a handheld instrument for projecting images onto a flat surface; usually a metal rod with a *prism* mounted on one end (see pp. 89–91).

CAMERA OBSCURA a way of projecting a scene onto a flat surface in a darkened room or box. The image produced is upside down and flipped left to right (see pp. 88–89).

CAVE PAINTING pictures made by ancient artists on the walls of caves.

CHARCOAL a drawing stick made from burned wood.

CIRCA (C.) approximately; as in "the artist was born *c*. 1500," meaning "the artist was born around 1500."

COLLAGE a work of art made by combining different images or objects together on a flat surface.

CUBISM an art movement that began in Paris in the early 20th century; artists Pablo Picasso and Georges Braque ignored the rules of *perspective* and combined many different points of view in a single picture.

FILM ROLL (or *roll of film*) a strip of coated plastic wound into a small cylinder and loaded in a camera. Once the photographs have been taken, the roll is sent to a laboratory to be developed.

FILM STILL a single image taken from a film—usually one *frame* from a longer sequence of frames.

HANDSCROLL a drawing or painting on a long, horizontal piece of paper; to look at the picture, you have to unroll it. Many examples can be found in ancient Chinese art.

ILLUSION something that looks real, but isn't actually there.

IMPRESSIONISM an art movement that began in France in the late 19th century. Artists wanted to give the *impression* of a scene, not just produce an exact copy of it. They made sketch-like pictures using marks or brushstrokes that some people complained looked unfinished.

LANDSCAPE a painting or photograph of an outdoor scene.

LENS (CAMERA) a curved piece of glass used in a camera to project an image onto a flat surface such as a *plate* or a *roll of film*.

OPEN AIR PAINTING a painting made outside in nature rather than in the artist's studio.

PALETTE a flat oval board, often made of wood, on which an artist mixes paint colors.

PERSPECTIVE a way of picturing a scene so that it appears to have distance and depth.

PIGMENT colored powder that is mixed with oil or water to make paint; artists mixed their own paints until the arrival of paint tubes in the 19th century.

PORTRAIT a picture of a person; a portrait can be a painting, photograph, or *sculpture*.

PRINT a work of art that can be reproduced many times. Usually, a picture is engraved or cut into a flat piece of wood or metal. This is then covered with ink so when paper is pressed against it, the picture is transferred. (Photographs are also known as *prints*.)

PRISM a transparent piece of glass that is used to reflect light.

SCULPTURE a *three-dimensional* piece of art, often made from stone, clay, or plaster.

SHUTTER in a camera, a device that moves to let in light and allows a photograph to be taken.

SILHOUETTE the dark outline produced when a person or object is placed in front of a beam of light.

STILL LIFE a painted arrangement of objects, such as a bowl of fruit.

THREE-DIMENSIONAL an object with height, depth, and width.

WOODBLOCK PRINT a *print* made from a piece of carved wood; particularly popular in Japanese art.

ENDNOTES

Full publication details for works cited in abbreviated form below can be found in the Bibliography.

CHAPTER 1

page 13: The task of a map-maker is to describe: Jerry Brotton, *A History of the World in Twelve Maps* (London and New York, 2012), pp. 10–12.

page 13: It's impossible to do this precisely: The impossibility was shown by Carl Friedrich Gauss in the 1820s, ibid., p. 12.

page 18: Van Gogh was one of the first artists: See Chris Stolwijk et al., *Vincent's Choice: The Musée Imaginaire of Van Gogh* (exh. cat., Amsterdam, 2003), pp. 110–12, 288–97.

page 21: That face is marvelously lit: In the context of DH's description of the Mona Lisa, it is worth noting that Leonardo was extremely interested in lighting. He recommends observing faces in dull weather and as evening falls, for soft shadows, and posing the model in a courtyard with black walls and a veil of cloth across the opening to the sky. Leonardo da Vinci, *Notebooks*, p. 222.

CHAPTER 2

page 29: Leonard da Vinci said that when he looked at the random shapes: Leonardo da Vinci, *Notebooks*, p. 173.

page 31: Chinese priest and painter Muqi: Laurence Sickman and Alexander Soper, *The Art and Architecture of China* (3rd edn, Harmondsworth, 1971), pp. 26–63.

page 34: Michelangelo had no work there to show him, but he was able to take his quill pen: Ascanio Condivi, "Life of Michelangelo Buonarroti," in Michelangelo, *Life, Letters, and Poetry*, selected and trans. with an introduction by George Bull (Oxford, 1987), pp. 19–20.

page 38: There are some wonderful Monet paintings of ice melting on the River Seine: See Annette Dixon, Carole McNamara and Charles Stuckey, *Monet at Vétheuil: The Turning Point* (exh. cat., Ann Arbor,

MI, 1998), pp. 41–86.

page 38: The winter of 1879–80 was one of the coldest: ibid., p. 78.

CHAPTER 3

page 44: Roman author Pliny the Elder wrote: J. J. Pollitt, *The Art of Ancient Greece: Sources and Documents* (Cambridge, 1990), p. 124.

page 44: "Silhouettes" were a cheap and popular type of portrait: Roy Sorensen, *Seeing Dark Things: The Philosophy of Shadows* (Oxford and New York, 2008), p. 26.

page 45: A silhouette is very distinctive: Animals and birds, as well as people, can recognize silhouettes, ibid., pp. 33–35.

page 48: Orson Welles, the actor playing Lime, was off set: Charles Drazin, *In Search of the Third Man* (London, 1999), p. 59.

page 50: There's a wonderful story of a competition between two ancient Greek artists: Pollitt, op. cit., pp. 149–50.

page 52: I think Caravaggio made his pictures by projecting images: For an advocacy of the idea Caravaggio might have pieced his compositions together without optical aids, see John L. Varriano, *Caravaggio: The Art of Realism* (University Park, PA, 2006), pp. 2–16. For an opposing view, see Clovis Whitfield, *Caravaggio's Eye* (London, 2011).

CHAPTER 5

page 74: Leonardo suggested painters should judge their works by looking at them in a flat mirror: Leonardo da Vinci, *Notebooks*, p. 221. Alberti made the same point: Alberti, *On Painting*, p. 83.

page 74: The shining shield: David Summers, *Vision, Reflection, and Desire in Western Painting* (Chapel Hill, NC, 2007), pp. 40–41.

page 76: Italian artist Parmigianino even had a special curved piece of wood made: Vasari, *Lives of the Painters, Sculptors and Architects*, vol. 1, p. 935.

page 78: It's a picture about a reflection:

For a thorough account of *Las Meninas*, see Jonathan Brown, *Velázquez: Painter and Courtier* (New Haven and London, 1986), pp. 256–64.

page 79: Some people think it's a reflection of the picture: ibid., p. 257.

CHAPTER 6

page 86: But he used a powerful lens: For a technical analysis of 17th-century lenses, see Giuseppe Molesini, "The optical quality of seventeenth-century lenses," in Wolfgang Lefèvre (ed.), *Inside the Camera Obscura— Optics and Art under the Spell of the Projected Image* (Berlin, 2007), pp. 117–27. See also, Tiemen Cocquyt, "The camera obscura and the availability of seventeenth century optics—some notes and an account of a test," in Lefèvre (ed.), op. cit., pp. 129–40.

page 86: The earliest telescopes were invented there, in 1608: On the question of 17th-century lenses, telescopes, and cameras, see Molesini, also Cocquyt and Wirth, in Lefèvre (ed.), op. cit.

page 86: Many different ideas have been suggested: See Wirth, in Lefèvre (ed.), op. cit., who reconstructs differing methods of using a lens to project images for Vermeer and Velázquez, and Steadman, *Vermeer's Camera*.

page 89: In 1807, the scientist William Hyde Wollaston: For an account of Wollaston, the invention of the camera lucida, and its use, see Larry J. Schaaf, *Out of the Shadows: Herschel, Talbot & the Invention of Photography* (New Haven and London, 1992), pp. 28–31.

page 90: It's my view that Ingres made these portraits … with the camera lucida: On Ingres and the camera lucida, see Hockney, *Secret Knowledge*, pp. 23 and 33.

page 94: It's no surprise that painters— like the French artist Edgar Degas—were fascinated with photography: On Degas and photography, see Dominique de Font-Réaulx, *Painting and Photography: 1839–1914* (Paris, 2012), pp. 277–82.

page 96: The painter Maurice Denis: Elizabeth W. Easton (ed.), *Snapshot: Painters and Photography, Bonnard to Vuillard* (New Haven and London, 2011), pp. 114–15.

page 96: It took two people to carry: Colin Ford, *Julia Margaret Cameron: 19th Century Photographer of Genius* (London, 2003), p. 41.

page 97: Photography changed again: Todd Gustavson, *500 Cameras: 170 Years of Photographic Innovation* (New York, 2011), pp. 224–32.

page 98: Piecing together different photographic images: Dawn Ades, Emily Butler, and Daniel F. Herrmann (eds), *Hannah Höch* (exh. cat., London and Munich, 2014), p. 161.

CHAPTER 7

page 102: In 1878, Eadweard Muybridge: Marta Braun, *Eadweard Muybridge* (London, 2010), pp. 133–58.

page 104: The first public film show: However, several other performances, in both the USA and Germany, are candidates for the honor of first public movie show, see André Gaudreault, *American Cinema, 1890–1909: Themes and Variations* (New Brunswick, NJ, 2009), pp. 3–6.

page 104: It was another French filmmaker, Georges Méliès: See the documentary film on Méliès, *The Extraordinary Voyage (Le voyage extraordinaire)*, directed by Serge Bromberg and Eric Lange, 2011.

BOOKS AND EXHIBITION CATALOGUES

Alberti, Leon Battista. *On Painting*, trans. with an introduction by John R. Spencer. London and New Haven: Yale University Press, 1966.

Edgerton, Samuel Y. *The Mirror, the Window, and the Telescope: How Renaissance Linear Perspective Changed our Vision of the Universe*. Ithaca: Cornell University Press, 2009.

Font-Réaulx, Dominique de. *Painting and Photography: 1839–1914*. Paris: Flammarion, 2012.

Gayford, Martin. *A Bigger Message: Conversations with David Hockney*. London and New York: Thames & Hudson, 2011.

Gombrich, E. H. *The Story of Art*, 16th edn. London: Phaidon, 1950; *The Heritage of Apelles*. Oxford: Phaidon, 1976.

Hibbard, Howard, *Caravaggio*. New York: Harper and Row Icon Editions, 1983.

Hockney, David. *Secret Knowledge: Rediscovering the Lost Techniques of the Old Masters*. London and New York: Thames & Hudson, 2001.

Kemp, Martin. *The Science of Art: Optical Themes in Western Art from Brunelleschi to Seurat*. New Haven and London: Yale University Press, 1990.

Leonardo da Vinci. *Notebooks*, selected by Irma A. Richter, ed. with an introduction by Thereza Wells. Oxford: Oxford University Press, 2008.

Pliny the Elder. *Natural History: A Selection*, trans. with an introduction by John F. Healy. London: Penguin Classics, 1991.

Schaaf, Larry J. *Out of the Shadows: Herschel, Talbot & the Invention of Photography*, New Haven and London: Yale University Press, 1992.

Scharf, Aaron. *Art and Photography*, rev. edn, Harmondsworth and Baltimore: Penguin, 1974.

Steadman, Phillip. *Vermeer's Camera: Uncovering the Truth Behind the Masterpieces*. Oxford: Oxford University Press, 2002.

Summers, David. *Vision, Reflection, and Desire in Western Painting*. Chapel Hill, NC: University of North Carolina Press, 2007.

Vasari, Giorgio. *The Lives of the Most Excellent Painters, Sculptors, and Architects*, trans. Gaston de Vere with an introduction by Philip Jacks. New York: Modern Library, 2006.

DOCUMENTARIES

A Day on the Grand Canal with the Emperor of China. Dir. Philip Haas. DVD. Milestone Films, 1988.

David Hockney's Secret Knowledge. Omnibus. Dir. and prod., Randall Wright. BBC1, London.

LIST OF ILLUSTRATIONS

and Wine Jar, from the House of Julia Felix, Pompeii, c. 70 CE. Fresco, Museo Archeologico Nazionale, Naples

page 51: Clara Peeters, Still Life with Fruit, Dead Birds, and a Monkey, date unknown. Oil on panel, 47.6 x 65.5 (18¾ x 25¾). Private collection

page 53: Caravaggio, The Taking of Christ, c. 1602. Oil on canvas, 133.5 × 169.5 (52½ × 66¾). National Gallery of Ireland, Dublin. age fotostock/Alamy Stock Photo

page 54: Caravaggio, The Supper at Emmaus, 1601. Oil on canvas, 141 × 196.2 (55½ × 77¼). National Gallery, London

page 55a: Caravaggio, The Incredulity of Saint Thomas, 1601–02. Oil on canvas, 107 × 146 (42⅛ × 57½). Sanssouci, Potsdam

page 55l: Caravaggio, The Taking of Christ (detail), c. 1602. Oil on canvas, 133.5 × 169.5 (52½ × 66¾). National Gallery of Ireland, Dublin. age fotostock/Alamy Stock Photo

page 55c: Caravaggio, The Supper at Emmaus (detail), 1601. Oil on canvas, 141 × 196.2 (55½ × 77¼). National Gallery, London

page 55r: Caravaggio, The Incredulity of Saint Thomas (detail), 1601–02. Oil on canvas, 107 × 146 (42⅛ × 57½). Sanssouci, Potsdam. Photo Gerhard Murza, Scala 2016, Florence/bpk, Berlin

page 58: David Hockney, The Second Marriage, 1963. Oil, gouache, and collage on canvas, 197.4 × 228.6 (77¾ × 90). National Gallery of Victoria, Melbourne. Photo National Gallery of Victoria, Melbourne. © David Hockney

page 59: Andrei Rublev, Holy Trinity (Troitsa), 1425–27. Tempera on wood, 141.5 × 114 (55¾ × 44⅞). The State Tretyakov Gallery, Moscow

page 60–61: Paolo Uccello, The Hunt in the Forest (detail), c. 1470. Tempera and oil, with traces of gold, on panel, 73.3 x 177 (29 x 69⅝). Ashmolean Museum, University of Oxford

page 62–63: Jan van Eyck, The Madonna with Canon van der Paele, 1436. Oil on wood, 122 × 157 (48 × 61). Groeningemuseum, Bruges. akg-images/Erich Lessing

page 64–65: David Hockney, Pearblossom Hwy., 11–18 April 1986 (second version), 1986. Photographic collage, 181.6 x 271.8 (71½ x 107). The J. Paul Getty Museum, Los Angeles. © David Hockney

page 66: Wang Hui, Kangxi Emperor's Southern Inspection Tour, Scroll Seven: Wuxi to Suzhou, 1689 (detail), 1689. Ink and color on silk, 67.7 × 2220 (26⅝ × 874). The Mactaggart Art Collection, Edmonton. Photo The Mactaggart Art Collection, University of Alberta Museums, Edmonton, Canada

page 67: Copy of Huang Kung-wang, Dwelling in the Fu-ch'un Mountains, 1347. Ink on paper, 33 x 636.9 (13 x 250¾). Original in National Palace Museum, Taipei. Photo Prudence Cuming Associates Ltd., London

page 68: Leonardo da Vinci, The Last Supper, 1494–99. Tempera on gesso, pitch and mastic, 460 × 880 (181⅛ × 346½). Santa Maria delle Grazie, Milan

page 69: Edward Hopper, Nighthawks, 1942. Oil on canvas, 84 × 152 (33⅛ × 59⅞). Art Institute of Chicago

page 70: Juan Gris, The Violin, 1916. Oil on wood, 105 x 73.6 (45½ x 29). Kunstmuseum, Basel

page 74: Eretria Painter, Seated woman holding a mirror, 430 BCE. Athenian red-figure amphoriskos, Ashmolean Museum, University of Oxford. Ashmolean Museum/Mary Evans

page 75: The Battle of Issus between Alexander the Great and Darius (detail) from the Alexander Mosaic from the House of the Faun, Pompeii, c. 315 BCE. Tesserae. Museo Archeologico Nazionale, Naples. Andrew Bargery/Alamy Stock Photo

page 76: Parmigianino, Self-Portrait in a Convex Mirror, c. 1523–24. Oil on poplar, diameter 24.4 (9⅝). Kunsthistorisches Museum, Vienna. Photo FineArt/Alamy Stock Photo

page 77: René Magritte, Not to be reproduced, 1937. Oil on canvas, 81 x 65 (31⅞ x 25⅝). Museum Boijmans van Beuningen, Rotterdam. © ADAGP, Paris and DACS, London 2017

page 78, 79: Diego Velázquez, Las Meninas, c. 1656. Oil on canvas, 318 × 276 (125¼ × 108⅝). Museo del Prado, Madrid page 81: David Hockney, *Untitled, 24 February 2011*, 2011. iPad Drawing. © David Hockney

page 82: Claude Monet, *Nymphéas*, 1905. Oil on canvas, 73 × 107 (28¾ × 42⅛). Private collection

page 83: David Hockney, *Study of Water, Phoenix, Arizona*, 1976. Colored crayon on paper, 45.7 × 49.8 (18 × 19⅝). Private collection. © David Hockney

page 87: Johannes Vermeer, *View of Houses in Delft*, known as *The Little Street*, c. 1658. Oil on canvas, 54.3 × 44 (21⅜ × 17⅜). Rijksmuseum, Amsterdam

page 88–89: Wenceslaus Hollar, *A View from St. Mary's, Southwark, Looking Toward Westminster* (detail), c. 1638. Pen and black ink over pencil on medium, slightly textured, cream wove paper, 13 × 30.8 (5⅛ × 12⅛). Yale Center for British Art, Paul Mellon Collection

page 90: Jean-Auguste-Dominique Ingres, *Portrait of Madame Louis-François Godinot, née Victoire-Pauline Thiollière de l'Isla*, 1829. Graphite, 21.9 x 16.5 (8½ x 6½). Collection of André Bromberg, Paris. Photo Sotheby's, Paris

page 91: David Hockney, *Maria Vasquez. London. 21 December 1999* (detail), 1999. Pencil, crayon, and gouache on gray paper using a camera lucida, 56.2 x 38.1 (22⅛ x 15). Photo Richard Schmidt. © David Hockney

page 92: William Henry Fox Talbot, *William Henry Fox Talbot (right)*

with assistants at their calotype production facility in Baker Street, Reading, Berkshire, 1846. Photo Pictorial Press Ltd/Alamy Stock Photo

page 93: Julia Margaret Cameron, *Sir John Herschel*, 1867. Albumen silver print from glass negative, 35.9 × 27.9 (14⅛ × 11)

page 94: André-Adolphe-Eugène Disdéri, *Prince Richard de Metternich and Princess Pauline de Metternich*, 1860. Carte-de-visite. Château de Compiègne, France. Photo RMN-Grand Palais (Domaine de Compiègne)/Gérard Blot

page 95: Edgar Degas, *Princess Pauline de Metternich*, c. 1865. Oil on canvas, 41 × 29 (16⅛ × 11⅜). National Gallery, London

page 96: Maurice Denis, *Two girls, wading in the sea, swinging little Madeleine, Perros-Guirec*, 1909. Gelatin silver print. Musée Maurice Denis, Saint-Germain-en-Laye. Photo Musée d'Orsay, Dist. RMN-Grand Palais/Patrice Schmidt

page 97: Henri Cartier-Bresson, *Place de l'Europe. Gare Saint Lazare*, 1932. © Henri Cartier-Bresson/ Magnum Photos

page 98: Hannah Höch, *Cut with the Kitchen Knife through the Last Weimar Beer-Belly Cultural Epoch in Germany*, 1919–1920. Photomontage and collage with watercolour, 114 x 90 (44⅞ × 35⅜). Staatliche Museen zu Berlin, Nationalgalerie. © DACS 2017

page 99: David Hockney, *4 Blue Stools*, 2014. Photographic drawing printed on paper, mounted on Dibond, edition of 25, 108 × 176.5 (42½ × 69½). Photo Richard Schmidt. © David Hockney

page 103: Eadweard Muybridge, *The Horse in Motion*, 1878

page 104: Still from Georges Méliès, *A Trip to the Moon*, 1902

page 105: Walt Disney Productions, still from *The Jungle Book*, 1967. © 1967 Walt Disney

page 107: Still from Charlie Chaplin, *City Lights*, 1931. United Artists/ Kobal/REX/Shutterstock

page 108: Victor Fleming, Still from *The Wizard of Oz*, 1939. Metro-Goldwyn-Mayer (now Warner Bros). © AF archive/Alamy Stock Photo

page 109: David Hockney, *The Four Seasons, Woldgate Woods (Spring 2011, Summer 2010, Autumn 2010, Winter 2010)*, 2010–2011, 36 digital videos synchronised and presented on 36 monitors. National Gallery of Victoria, Melbourne. © David Hockney

page 112: ustwo Games, *Monument Valley*, 2014. © ustwo Games 2014

page 115: Fred Morley, *The London Milkman*, 1940. Fred Morley/Getty Images